T0274916

MOCKTAILS

A COLLECTION OF
NO-PROOF COCKTAILS

CIDER MILL
PRESS

BOOK
PUBLISHERS

CONTENTS

INTRODUCTION

In a world where we are constantly overwhelmed with choices, it is odd that the options are so narrow when the time comes to turn away from the workday and unwind with a beverage—in most instances, this void will be filled by some sort of alcoholic drink. And, while these beverages are no doubt delicious and do take the edge off, they also come with adverse effects, affecting sleep and other important health factors.

Because of the hold that cocktails, beer, and wine have on our brains when we want to relax with a drink, we tend to lose sight of what we're really craving, which is something that refreshes, revitalizes, and tastes great.

As you'll see, you don't need booze to check those three boxes. We're all familiar with the concept of a mocktail—a tasty blend of ingredients that contains no alcohol. But not too many of us have gone further than this modest acquaintance and learned just how wonderful the world of zero-proof drinks can be. This book seeks to remedy that, collecting refreshing and refined drinks so that there's something for everyone, whether you're looking for a beverage that can impersonate your favorite cocktail or one that uses imagination and bespoke ingredients to produce an innovative elixir. And the number of delicious nonalcoholic blends available is growing daily, as companies such as Lyre's, El Guapo, Töst, and others are crafting quality nonalcoholic options to match the spirits and bitters whose flavors were previously thought to be impossible to replicate.

These companies and the delicious recipes collected here prove that booze is no longer the only name in the refreshment game—the time has come to rethink how and what you drink.

CLASSICS

From the Shirley Temple to the Arnold Palmer, most will be familiar with the drinks in this chapter. But there's also a number of mocktails that do a bang-on impersonation of some of the most famous cocktails in the world. As these can be a good place to start for the individual who is uncertain about where to begin in the zero-proof world, we've placed them beside the more-familiar standbys.

HOT BUTTERED RUM

GLASSWARE: MUG
GARNISH: CINNAMON STICK

Tasting notes: spicy, rich, creamy, comforting

A drink made for those nights in late autumn when you can feel Father Winter around the corner.

---

1 tablespoon unsalted butter

1 teaspoon brown sugar

Dash of Cinnamon Syrup (see page 191)

Dash of freshly grated nutmeg

Dash of orange zest

2 oz. vanilla ice cream

4 oz. hot water

1   Place the butter, brown sugar, syrup, nutmeg, and orange zest in the mug and muddle.

2   Add the ice cream, top with the hot water, and stir to combine.

3   Taste, adjust the seasoning as needed, garnish with the cinnamon stick, and enjoy.

IF YOU LIKE PIÑA COLADAS

GLASSWARE: HURRICANE GLASS
GARNISH: PINEAPPLE CHUNK

Tasting notes: tropical, refreshing, sweet, sour

Just as delicious as the tiki classic, and just as capable of taking the edge off.

---

1 oz. cream of coconut

3 oz. pineapple juice

1 oz. Coffee Syrup (see page 189)

1   Place all of the ingredients in a blender, add 5 oz. crushed ice, and puree until smooth.

2   Pour the drink into the Hurricane glass, garnish with the pineapple chunk, and enjoy.

If You Like Piña Coladas, see page 11

SHIRLEY TEMPLE

GLASSWARE: HIGHBALL GLASS
GARNISH: MARASCHINO CHERRY

Tasting notes: sweet, spicy, refreshing

Originated as a means of refreshing the mocktail's namesake when she was too young to participate in the activities of her fellow megastars, this serve has since stood the test of time like no other mocktail.

6 oz. ginger ale

½ oz. Grenadine
(see page 197)

½ oz. fresh lime juice

1 Place all of the ingredients in the highball glass, add ice, and stir until chilled.

2 Garnish with the maraschino cherry and enjoy.

ROY ROGERS

GLASSWARE: HIGHBALL GLASS
GARNISH: MARASCHINO CHERRY

Tasting notes: sweet, syrupy, tart

Another classic celebrity-inspired drink built around soda and Grenadine, but here the latter has an even harder task to pull off, balancing out the syrupy sweetness of cola. Luckily, this homemade version does the job.

---

6 oz. cola

½ oz. Grenadine
(see page 197)

½ oz. fresh lime juice

1   Place all of the ingredients in the highball glass, add ice, and stir until chilled.

2   Garnish with the maraschino cherry and enjoy.

FUZZY NAVEL

GLASSWARE: CHAMPAGNE FLUTE
GARNISH: PEACH WEDGE

Tasting notes: sweet, tart, floral

Celebratory, eye-catching, and delicious—this is a drink that can work any time of day, in any situation.

---

1 oz. peach nectar

3 oz. orange juice

2 dashes of El Guapo Love Potion bitters

1   Place the ingredients in a cocktail shaker, fill it two-thirds of the way with ice, and shake vigorously until chilled.

2   Strain over ice into the Champagne flute, garnish with the peach wedge, and enjoy.

MUDSLIDE

GLASSWARE: ROCKS GLASS
GARNISH: WHIPPED CREAM

Tasting notes: rich, sweet, nutty

The tinge of apricot in Monin's amaretto syrup takes this beloved dessert drink to heights its boozy brother can't reach.

---

1 oz. heavy cream

2 scoops of vanilla ice cream

Dash of Monin amaretto syrup

1 oz. Chocolate Ganache (see page 192)

1   Place the heavy cream, ice cream, syrup, and ganache in a blender and puree until smooth.

2   Pour the drink over ice into the rocks glass, garnish with whipped cream, and enjoy.

LIME RICKEY

GLASSWARE: HIGHBALL GLASS
GARNISH: LIME WEDGE

Tasting notes: tart, effervescent, refreshing

The bit of sodium in club soda lifts the other elements in this simple, delightful refresher.

---

1 oz. Simple Syrup (see page 193)

1 oz. fresh lime juice

4 oz. club soda

1 Place the syrup and lime juice in a highball glass and stir to combine.

2 Add ice and top with the club soda.

3 Garnish with the lime wedge and enjoy.

MOJITO

GLASSWARE: TUMBLER
GARNISH: FRESH MINT, LIME WEDGE

Tasting notes: herbal, refreshing, sweet, tart

A mocktail that has something to grab everyone: freshness, spice, sweetness, and some citric tartness.

---

1 tablespoon caster (superfine) sugar

½ oz. fresh lime juice

Handful of fresh mint leaves

4 oz. ginger ale

4 oz. cola

1 Place the sugar and lime juice in the tumbler and stir until the sugar has dissolved.

2 Add the mint leaves and muddle.

3 Add ice, the ginger ale and cola and gently stir to combine.

4 Garnish with fresh mint and the lime wedge and enjoy.

BLOODY MARY

Tasting notes: spicy, revitalizing, umami

Since vodka has a neutral flavor, you aren't missing anything when you go with this nonalcoholic version.

Dash of black pepper, plus more for the rim

½ oz. fresh lime wedge

½ oz. olive brine

2 dashes of horseradish

3 drops of Worcestershire sauce

3 dashes of hot sauce

2 dashes of celery salt

6 oz. tomato juice

1 Wet the rim of the tumbler and coat it with black pepper.

2 Add the remaining ingredients to a cocktail shaker, fill it two-thirds of the way with ice, and shake vigorously until chilled.

3 Add ice to the tumbler and strain the cocktail over it.

4 Garnish with whatever your heart desires and enjoy.

PIMM'S CUP

GLASSWARE: HIGHBALL GLASS
GARNISH: CUCUMBER SLICES, LEMON WHEEL

Tasting notes: fruity, floral, herbal, summery

This is a good one to turn into a large batch drink for a summer barbecue. If that sounds appealing, just maintain the ratios and multiply the amounts by the number of servings you want to make.

---

4 fresh mint leaves

2 oz. sparkling lemonade

1 oz. ginger ale

1 oz. cola

½ oz. orange juice

½ oz. fresh lemon juice

2 drops of El Guapo Love Potion bitters

1   Place the mint leaves in the highball glass and muddle.

2   Add ice and the remaining ingredients and stir to combine.

3   Garnish with the cucumber slices and lemon wheel and enjoy.

MOSCOW MULE

GLASSWARE: COPPER MUG
GARNISH: LIME WEDGE, FRESH MINT

Tasting notes: sweet, spicy, sour

A big part of embracing nonalcoholic beverages is developing a taste for ginger beer—this refreshing drink makes that effortless.

1 oz. fresh lime juice

1 oz. Honey & Ginger Syrup (see page 190)

6 oz. ginger beer

1 Place the ingredients in the copper mug, fill it with crushed ice, and gently stir to combine.

2 Garnish with the lime wedge and fresh mint and enjoy.

Moscow Mule, see page 29

STRAWBERRY DAIQUIRI

GLASSWARE: HURRICANE GLASS
GARNISH: STRAWBERRY

Tasting notes: sweet, tart, tropical, frozen

Just as decadent and delicious as it was when your parents humored you and let you order one those rare times you went out to a restaurant to eat.

2 oz. Lemon-Lime Juice (see page 194)

½ oz. orange juice

¼ oz. Simple Syrup (see page 193)

½ cup hulled strawberries

1 Place all of the ingredients in a blender, add 5 oz. crushed ice, and puree until smooth.

2 Pour the drink into the Hurricane glass, garnish with the strawberry, and enjoy.

LONG ISLAND ICED TEA

GLASSWARE: DOUBLE ROCKS GLASS
GARNISH: LEMON WHEEL, FRESH ROSEMARY

Tasting notes: herbal, refreshing, sweet

The name will put some off, but this one resides out on the calming beaches of Montauk rather than the grind of the expressway.

2 oz. iced tea

2 oz. lemonade

2 oz. cola

1   Place the iced tea and lemonade in a cocktail shaker, fill it two-thirds of the way with ice, and shake vigorously until chilled.

2   Strain over ice into the double rocks glass and top with the cola.

3   Garnish with the lemon wheel and rosemary and enjoy.

ARNOLD PALMER

GLASSWARE: HIGHBALL GLASS
GARNISH: LEMON SLICE

Tasting notes: refreshing, sweet, tart

A drink so good it ensures that The King's legacy will live on for centuries.

3 oz. lemonade

3 oz. sweetened iced tea

1 Add ice to the highball glass, add the lemonade, and stir until chilled.

2 Slowly pour the iced tea over the back of a spoon so that it gradually filters down into the lemonade.

3 Garnish with the lemon slice and enjoy.

MINT JULEP

GLASSWARE: TIN CUP OR HIGHBALL GLASS
GARNISH: FRESH MINT

Tasting notes: effervescent, refreshing, sweet, herbal

*Take a cue from this one: when you have a drink featuring
ingredients that head in a number of directions, saline solution
is the key to get them pulling together.*

---

6 fresh mint leaves

**1 teaspoon confectioners'
sugar**

½ oz. fresh lemon juice

½ oz. water

**½ oz. 10 Percent Saline
Solution (see page 195)**

3 oz. ginger ale

1   Place the mint, confectioners'
    sugar, lemon juice, water, and
    saline solution in the chosen
    glass and muddle.

2   Add crushed ice and the ginger ale
    and stir until chilled.

3   Top with more crushed ice, garnish
    with fresh mint, and enjoy.

COSMOPOLITAN

GLASSWARE: COCKTAIL GLASS
GARNISH: ORANGE TWIST OR LIME WEDGE

Tasting notes: tart, sweet, bright

The splash of Sweet & Sour provides this drink with a wonderful mouthfeel and the touch of sweetness it needs.

---

4 oz. cranberry juice

½ oz. fresh lime juice

Splash of Sweet & Sour (see page 196)

1   Place all of the ingredients in a cocktail shaker, fill it two-thirds of the way with ice, and shake vigorously until combined.

2   Strain into the cocktail glass, garnish with the orange twist or lime wedge, and enjoy.

SANGRIA

GLASSWARE: WINEGLASSES
GARNISH: LEMON WHEELS

Tasting notes: fruity, sour, sweet

White or red grape juice works well as the foundation for this fruity mélange.

---

10 oz. grape juice

6 oz. apple juice

4 oz. orange juice

2 oz. fresh lemon juice

2 oz. fresh lime juice

1 apple, peeled, cored, and diced

1 orange, peeled and sliced thin

1 cup blackberries

4 oz. club soda

1 Place all of the ingredients, except for the club soda, in a large container, stir to combine, and cover the container. Chill in the refrigerator overnight.

2 Pour the mixture into a punch bowl, add the club soda, and gently stir to combine.

3 Serve over ice in wineglasses and garnish with lemon wheels.

FRUITY
PLEASERS

As no one has a flair for flavor quite like Mother Nature, a straightforward blend of juices is oftentimes the surest way to craft a drink that will revitalize, refresh, and delight the taste buds. From that strong starting point, we've fortified those fruitful mixtures with bespoke syrups and other intriguing tinctures to create a series of memorable serves.

BLACKBIRD

GLASSWARE: ROCKS GLASS
GARNISH: FRESH MINT

Tasting notes: tropical, nutty, rich, tart

The Cashew Orgeat inclines this drink toward decadence, but the trio of sour ingredients cuts against this quality beautifully.

¾ oz. fresh lime juice

¾ oz. fresh lemon juice

1 oz. Cashew Orgeat (see page 198)

5 fresh blackberries

3 oz. Bottlegreen blackberry, apple & sloe cordial

1 Place the juices, orgeat, and blackberries in a cocktail shaker and muddle.

2 Add ice and shake vigorously until chilled.

3 Double strain over crushed ice into the rocks glass and top with the cordial.

4 Garnish with the fresh mint and enjoy.

LITTLE RED SHOES

GLASSWARE: ROCKS GLASS
GARNISH: POMEGRANATE SEEDS

Tasting notes: tart, sweet, bright

Pomegranate juice looks sweet, but it has a deep sourness that is irresistible once you get a taste for it.

---

3 oz. pomegranate juice

2 oz. fresh lime juice

1 oz. fresh orange juice

⅔ oz. Simple Syrup (see page 193)

1   Place all of the ingredients in a cocktail shaker, fill it two-thirds of the way with ice, and shake vigorously until chilled.

2   Strain over ice into the rocks glass, garnish with the pomegranate seeds, and enjoy.

CHERRY LIMEADE

GLASSWARE: HIGHBALL GLASS
GARNISH: LIME WEDGE

Tasting notes: sour, fruity, rich

A black cherry juice that is not made from concentrate will provide the best results here.

---

2 oz. black cherry juice

1 oz. Grenadine (see page 197)

1 oz. fresh lime juice

½ oz. Simple Syrup (see page 193)

½ oz. 10 Percent Saline Solution (see page 195)

1   Place all of the ingredients in a cocktail shaker, fill it two-thirds of the way with ice, and shake vigorously until chilled.

2   Strain over ice into the highball glass, garnish with the lime wedge, and enjoy.

OPEN RHYTHMS

GLASSWARE: HURRICANE GLASS
GARNISH: ORANGE WHEEL

Tasting notes: sour, refreshing, bright, berries

Blood orange juice is sweeter than most citrus, and it also carries strawberry and raspberry notes that are welcome additions here.

---

2 oz. orange juice

2 oz. fresh blood orange juice

Splash of Grenadine (see page 197)

1   Place the juices in a cocktail shaker, fill it two-thirds of the way with ice, and shake vigorously until chilled.

2   Pour the contents of the shaker into the Hurricane glass, add the Grenadine, and let it filter slowly through the drink.

3   Garnish with the orange wheel and enjoy.

NEW MOON

GLASSWARE: ROCKS GLASS
GARNISH: LIME WEDGE

Tasting notes: sour, spicy, floral, refreshing

The floral notes present in white grapefruit juice add necessary depth to this sour-and-spicy drink.

Salt, for the rim

1 oz. fresh lemon juice

1 oz. fresh lime juice

1 oz. white grapefruit juice

½ oz. Ginger Syrup (see page 199)

½ oz. Simple Syrup (see page 193)

1   Wet the rim of the rocks glass and coat it with salt.

2   Place the remaining ingredients in a cocktail shaker, fill it two-thirds of the way with ice, and shake vigorously until chilled.

3   Fill the glass with ice and strain the mocktail into the glass.

4   Garnish with the lime wedge and enjoy.

New Moon, see page 53

CORDILLERA

GLASSWARE: HIGHBALL GLASS
GARNISH: NONE

Tasting notes: tropical, vegetal, creamy, effervescent

The syrup boosts the cucumber flavor enough to prevent it from being drowned out by the cantaloupe.

½ cucumber, peeled and diced

½ cup chopped cantaloupe

½ oz. Cucumber Syrup (see page 201)

3 oz. club soda

1 Place the cucumber, cantaloupe, and syrup in a blender, add 3 oz. crushed ice, and puree until smooth.

2 Pour the puree into the highball glass, add the club soda, gently stir to combine, and enjoy.

SUNSHINE HOLIDAY

GLASSWARE: HIGHBALL GLASS
GARNISH: LEMON WHEELS, FRESH ROSEMARY

Tasting notes: sweet, sour, herbal

Spiking lemonade with the sharp, piney flavor of rosemary is the key to keeping its sweet side from becoming cloying after a couple of sips.

4 oz. lemonade

1 oz. Rosemary Syrup (see page 202)

½ oz. Grenadine (see page 197)

1 Place all of the ingredients in a cocktail shaker, fill it two-thirds of the way with ice, and shake vigorously until chilled.

2 Strain over ice into the highball glass, garnish with lemon wheels and fresh rosemary, and enjoy.

BAJA LEMONADE

GLASSWARE: ROCKS GLASS
GARNISH: LEMON WHEELS, FRESH ROSEMARY

Tasting notes: summery, tropical, sweet, sour

Coco López and Reàl are both strong options when shopping for cream of coconut.

---

5 oz. lemonade

1 oz. cream of coconut

Splash of agave nectar

1   Place the lemonade, cream of coconut, agave, and rosemary in a cocktail shaker, fill it two-thirds of the way with ice, and shake vigorously until chilled.

2   Double strain over ice into the rocks glass, garnish with the lemon wheel and rosemary, and enjoy.

...made, see page 59

WHISTLING IN TONGUES

Tasting notes: tropical, bright, fruity

While many fruits partner well with kiwi, apple stands above them all.

Salt, for the rim

1½ oz. apple juice

¾ oz. fresh lime juice

¼ cup peeled and diced kiwi

½ oz. Simple Syrup (see page 193)

¾ oz. fresh orange juice

1 Wet the rim of the rocks glass and coat it with salt.

2 Place the remaining ingredients in a blender, add 5 oz. crushed ice, and puree until smooth.

3 Pour the drink into the rocks glass, garnish with the slice of kiwi, and enjoy.

DEEP SKY

GLASSWARE: HIGHBALL GLASS
GARNISH: NONE

Tasting notes: tart, tropical, refreshing

A drink that shows the wisdom of always having some frozen passion fruit chunks on hand—once you do, a delicious, deeply-flavored drink is always right around the corner.

---

3 oz. passion fruit puree

1 oz. fresh lime juice

½ oz. fresh orange juice

½ oz. agave nectar

1 Place all of the ingredients in a blender, add 5 oz. crushed ice, and puree until smooth.

2 Pour the drink into the highball glass and enjoy.

A WALK IN THE PARK

GLASSWARE: NICK & NORA GLASS
GARNISH: MANGO SLICE

Tasting notes: summery, sour, tropical, piney

Floral, foresty, fresh, and revitalizing, any drink centered around mango will be a crowd-pleaser.

1¼ oz. mango puree

¼ oz. Simple Syrup (see page 193)

½ oz. fresh orange juice

½ oz. fresh lime juice

1 Place all of the ingredients in a cocktail shaker, fill it two-thirds of the way with ice, and shake vigorously until chilled.

2 Strain over ice into the Nick & Nora glass, garnish with the slice of mango, and enjoy.

CHRYSALIS

GLASSWARE: HIGHBALL GLASS
GARNISH: LEMON WHEEL, FRESH MINT

Tasting notes: refreshing, tropical, herbal, anise

A serve that will leave you feeling reborn on a hot summer day.

---

2 oz. water, chilled

2 oz. pineapple juice

½ oz. fresh lemon juice

¼ oz. Basil Syrup (see page 200)

1   Place all of the ingredients in a cocktail shaker, fill it two-thirds of the way with ice, and shake vigorously until chilled.

2   Strain over ice into the highball glass, garnish with the lemon wheel and fresh mint, and enjoy.

STRAWBERRY & BASIL LEMONADE

GLASSWARE: HIGHBALL GLASS
GARNISH: FRESH BASIL

Tasting notes: sweet, herbal, sour, bright

Strawberries and soft herbs like basil have an uncanny affinity for one another.

---

1 oz. Basil Syrup (see page 200)

2 oz. iced strawberry tea

1 oz. fresh lemon juice

1 teaspoon 10 Percent Saline Solution (see page 195)

1 Place all of the ingredients in a cocktail shaker, fill it two-thirds of the way with ice, and shake vigorously until chilled.

2 Strain over ice into the highball glass, garnish with fresh basil, and enjoy.

QUIVERING IN TIME

GLASSWARE: TUMBLER GLASS
GARNISH: FRESH THYME

Tasting notes: sweet, floral, earthy

Peach nectar can be a touch on the sweet side, but bracing it with the earthy qualities of both the tea and thyme makes this trait a strong suit.

---

2 oz. peach nectar

1 oz. iced peach tea

1 oz. Thyme Syrup (see page 203)

½ oz. fresh lemon juice

1   Place all of the ingredients in a cocktail shaker, fill it two-thirds of the way with ice, and shake vigorously until chilled.

2   Strain over ice into the tumbler, garnish with fresh thyme, and enjoy.

VACATION FROM MY MIND

GLASSWARE: ROCKS GLASS
GARNISH: FRESH BLUEBERRIES

Tasting notes: fruity, tart, bright, refreshing

Iced strawberry tea is a secret weapon when it comes to making mocktails, as it provides considerable berry flavor without also adding the sweetness that can throw a drink out of balance.

---

1 oz. iced strawberry tea

2 oz. blueberry juice

1 oz. Raspberry Syrup (see page 204)

1 oz. cranberry juice

1 oz. fresh lime juice

1   Place all of the ingredients in a cocktail shaker, fill it two-thirds of the way with ice, and shake vigorously until chilled.

2   Strain over crushed ice into the rocks glass, garnish with the blueberries, and enjoy.

WHAT'S UP DOC?

GLASSWARE: FOOTED PILSNER GLASS
GARNISH: CARROT GREENS

Tasting notes: vegetal, bright, spicy

The beguiling flavor of black currant juice, which is something like a blend of tropical fruits and berries, keys this surprisingly successful amalgam.

---

1 oz. black currant juice

½ oz. Bali Spice Syrup (see page 212)

¾ oz. fresh lemon juice

¾ oz. carrot juice

½ oz. orange juice

¼ oz. Ginger Syrup (see page 199)

¼ oz. maple syrup

1 Place all of the ingredients in a cocktail shaker, fill it two-thirds of the way with ice, and shake vigorously until chilled.

2 Strain over crushed ice into the footed pilsner glass, garnish with the carrot greens, and enjoy.

MILK BEACH

GLASSWARE: ROCKS GLASS
GARNISH: LAVENDER BUDS, LEMON WHEEL

Tasting notes: tropical, revitalizing, floral

A drink that you can easily sip all day while sitting in the sun.

---

2 oz. coconut water

1 oz. fresh lemon juice

1 oz. Lavender Syrup (see page 205)

2 dashes of El Guapo Polynesian Kiss bitters

1 Place all of the ingredients in a cocktail shaker, fill it two-thirds of the way with ice, and shake vigorously until chilled.

2 Strain over ice into the rocks glass, garnish with the lavender buds and lemon wheel, and enjoy.

Milk Beach, see page 77

OVER THE RAINBOW

GLASSWARE: HIGHBALL GLASS
GARNISH: ORANGE WHEEL

Tasting notes: tangy, sour, herbal

Getting serious about stepping up your mocktail game means upping your familiarity with the sweet, vinegar–based tonics known as shrubs. You can tailor any shrub to your own tastes, but for a basic recipe, simply add equal parts fruit or vegetable, sugar, and vinegar to a saucepan, boil for 5 to 10 minutes, let cool, and strain. Once you get comfortable with making them, experiment with adding accents, like the thyme here.

---

2 oz. iced hibiscus raspberry tea

½ oz. Raspberry & Thyme Shrub (see page 207)

½ oz. grapefruit juice

2 dashes of El Guapo Love Potion bitters

1 Place all of the ingredients in a cocktail shaker, fill it two-thirds of the way with ice, and shake vigorously until chilled.

2 Strain over ice into the highball glass, garnish with the orange wheel, and enjoy.

IDOL EYES

GLASSWARE: HIGHBALL GLASS
GARNISH: LIME WEDGE

Tasting notes: summery, tart, bright, tropical

El Guapo's Love Potion bitters feature a swirl of floral aromatics such as chamomile, orange blossom, jasmine, lavender, and hibiscus, making them a good fit for fruity punches such as this.

---

2 oz. cranberry juice

2 oz. grapefruit juice

1 oz. Banana Syrup (see page 208)

6 drops of El Guapo Love Potion bitters

1½ oz. Passion Fruit Honey (see page 209)

1   Place all of the ingredients in a cocktail shaker, fill it two-thirds of the way with ice, and shake vigorously until chilled.

2   Strain over ice into the highball glass, garnish with the lime wedge, and enjoy.

EASE YOURSELF AND GLIDE

GLASSWARE: HIGHBALL GLASS
GARNISH: NONE

Tasting notes: vanilla, tropical, spicy, bright

Orgeat (it's pronounced "ore-zha") is a French almond-based syrup that is available at most liquor stores and supermarkets, but a homemade version is best—not as sweet, and more complex.

---

2 oz. carrot, turmeric & ginger juice

1 oz. Orgeat (see page 210)

1 oz. fresh lime juice

1 oz. guava nectar

1   Place all of the ingredients in a cocktail shaker, fill it two-thirds of the way with ice, and shake vigorously until chilled.

2   Strain over crushed ice into the highball glass and enjoy.

LIQUID SUNSHINE

GLASSWARE: HIGHBALL GLASS
GARNISH: BRÛLÉED PINEAPPLE (SEE RECIPE), FRESH MINT

Tasting notes: tart, sweet, floral

The aroma of the caramelized pineapple garnish will brand each sip of this cocktail into your memory.

---

1 oz. fresh orange juice

¼ oz. fresh lime juice

1 oz. passion fruit puree

½ oz. grapefruit juice

½ oz. Hibiscus Syrup (see page 211)

6 drops of El Guapo Love Potion bitters

1 Place the orange juice in a blender and pulse to "fluff" the juice. Set the orange juice aside.

2 Build the cocktail in a highball glass, adding the remaining ingredients in the order they are listed. Fill the glass with crushed ice, leaving ½ inch of space for the orange juice.

3 Slowly pour the fluffed orange juice over the crushed ice.

4 Garnish the cocktail with the Brûléed Pineapple and fresh mint and enjoy.

Brûléed Pineapple: Simply place some sugar in a dish, roll a pineapple wedge in the sugar until it is coated, and then use a kitchen torch to brulée the pineapple.

WATERMELON MAN

GLASSWARE: TUMBLER
GARNISH: FRESH BASIL

Tasting notes: summery, refreshing, anise

The basil and lime juice provide the refreshment, allowing you to fully appreciate the watermelon's pleasantly bittersweet character.

---

1 oz. Basil Syrup (see page 200)

1½ cups watermelon cubes

1 oz. fresh lime juice

1   Place all of the ingredients in a blender, add 5 oz. crushed ice, and puree until smooth.

2   Pour the drink into the tumbler, garnish with fresh basil, and enjoy.

Watermelon Man, see page 87

THE VIOLET HOUR

GLASSWARE: COCKTAIL GLASS
GARNISH: FRESH MINT

Tasting notes: tropical, floral, spicy, fruity

The cardamom and elderflower syrup allow lychee's floral finish to come through crystal clear.

½ oz. lychee nectar

½ oz. peach nectar

½ oz. mango puree

¼ oz. Monin elderflower syrup

½ oz. fresh lemon juice

⅓ oz. ginger juice

Pinch of ground cardamom

2 dashes of El Guapo Holiday Pie bitters

1 Chill the cocktail glass in the freezer.

2 Place all of the ingredients in a cocktail shaker, fill it two-thirds of the way with ice, and shake vigorously until chilled.

3 Double strain into the chilled cocktail glass, garnish with fresh mint, and enjoy.

THE GREEN RAY

GLASSWARE: WINEGLASS
GARNISH: NONE

Tasting notes: rich, revitalizing, tropical

A combination of syrups rounds off all of the edges in this well-balanced drink.

½ oz. Molasses Syrup (see page 213)

1 oz. aloe vera juice

¾ oz. fresh lime juice

¾ oz. Demerara Syrup (see page 214)

1 oz. kiwi puree

¼ oz. fresh lemon juice

1 Place all of the ingredients in a blender, add 3 oz. crushed ice, and puree until smooth.

2 Pour the drink into the wineglass, top with more crushed ice, and enjoy.

DESERT RAIN

GLASSWARE: HIGHBALL GLASS
GARNISH: WATERMELON CHUNK

Tasting notes: herbal, tart, earthy

A drink that will have you reveling in Mother Nature's exceptional flair for flavor.

1½ cups watermelon cubes

½ cucumber, peeled and diced

8 fresh mint leaves, torn

1 oz. fresh lemon juice

½ oz. Agave Syrup (see page 206)

1 oz. iced prickly pear tea

1 oz. aloe vera juice

1 Place the watermelon and cucumber in a blender and puree until smooth.

2 Strain the puree into a cocktail shaker, add ice and the remaining ingredients, and shake vigorously until chilled.

3 Strain over crushed ice into the highball glass, garnish with the watermelon chunk, and enjoy.

Desert Rain, see page 93

PANDA LATINO

GLASSWARE: DOUBLE ROCKS GLASS
GARNISH: KIWI SLICE, FRESH ROSEMARY

Tasting notes: herbal, umami, floral

A potent herbal tea jumps out in front flavorwise, but the other ingredients rally to provide this serve a spectacular finish.

---

1 kiwi, peeled

1⅓ oz. Herb Tea (see page 215)

⅔ oz. Bottlegreen elderflower cordial

⅔ oz. fresh lemon juice

⅓ teaspoon freshly grated Parmesan cheese

1   Place all of the ingredients in a mason jar and use an immersion blender to emulsify the mixture.

2   Fill the double rocks glass with crushed ice and pour the drink over it.

3   Top the drink with more crushed ice, garnish with the slice of kiwi and fresh rosemary, and enjoy.

CHASIN' THE SUNSHINE

GLASSWARE: ROCKS GLASS
GARNISH: CRUSHED CINNAMON STICKS

Tasting notes: creamy, spicy, vanilla

The horchata takes the sting out of a trio of very spicy elements, allowing their complex flavors to shine.

½ oz. Ginger Syrup (see page 199)

1 oz. Thai Chile Shrub (see page 216)

2½ oz. Pear & Cardamom Horchata (see page 217)

½ oz. fresh lime juice

Dash of El Guapo Fuego bitters

1   Place all of the ingredients in a cocktail shaker, fill it two-thirds of the way with ice, and shake vigorously until chilled.

2   Strain over crushed ice into the rocks glass, garnish with the cinnamon sticks, and enjoy.

COFFEE
& TEA

As their true devotees know, coffee and tea are no slouches in the flavor department, providing as many if not more elements for the taste buds to be tantalized by than any offering from the world of spirits. This natural complexity makes them perfect ingredients to provide the foundation for a drink that is as refreshing and refined as anything available at a craft cocktail bar.

ON A MISTY MORNING

GLASSWARE: TUMBLER
GARNISH: NONE

Tasting notes: spicy, bitter, earthy, revitalizing

A mocktail that has the aesthetics to match its bold, memorable flavor.

---

2 slices of jalapeño chile pepper

½ oz. fresh lime juice

1 teaspoon 10 Percent Saline Solution (see page 195)

2¼ teaspoons matcha powder

1 oz. iced ginger tea

1½ oz. iced green tea

½ oz. Simple Syrup (see page 193)

1 Place the jalapeño and lime juice in a cocktail shaker and muddle.

2 Add ice and the remaining ingredients and shake vigorously until chilled.

3 Double strain over ice into the tumbler and enjoy.

MOMENT TO MOMENT

GLASSWARE: COCKTAIL GLASS
GARNISH: CHOCOLATE-COVERED ESPRESSO BEANS

Tasting notes: rich, creamy, sweet

To make the most of the chocolatey flavor here, look for coffee beans from South or Central America that feature a medium-dark roast.

---

3 oz. freshly brewed coffee

1 teaspoon honey

2 oz. heavy cream

1 teaspoon Chocolate Ganache (see page 192)

1 While the espresso or coffee is still hot, stir the honey into it. Chill the mixture in the refrigerator.

2 Place the sweetened espresso or coffee, heavy cream, and ganache in a cocktail shaker and shake vigorously until combined.

3 Double strain into the cocktail glass, garnish with the chocolate-covered espresso beans, and enjoy.

CORCOVADO

GLASSWARE: ROCKS GLASS
GARNISH: ORANGE TWIST

Tasting notes: earthy, nutty, woody

El Guapo's Chicory Pecan bitters will transport you to a quiet balcony in New Orleans on a bright, cool morning.

---

2 oz. espresso, at room temperature

2 dashes of El Guapo Chicory Pecan bitters

¼ oz. Rich Simple Syrup (see page 218)

1   Place all of the ingredients in a cocktail shaker, fill it two-thirds of the way with ice, and shake vigorously until chilled.

2   Strain over a large ice cube into the rocks glass, garnish with the orange twist, and enjoy.

CHAI CIDER

GLASSWARE: MUG
GARNISH: CINNAMON STICK

Tasting notes: spicy, floral, anise

Fans of mulled cider know how well it takes on spice, and this chai-inclined blend takes full advantage of this ability.

---

8 oz. apple cider

1-inch piece of fresh ginger, peeled and chopped

2 cinnamon sticks

4 whole cloves

4 cardamom pods, smashed

4 whole peppercorns

1 star anise pod

1 Place all of the ingredients in a medium saucepan and bring to a boil over medium heat.

2 Reduce the heat so that the mixture simmers and cook for 15 to 20 minutes.

3 Strain the drink into the mug, garnish with the cinnamon stick, and enjoy.

INTO THE WOODS

GLASSWARE: DOUBLE ROCKS GLASS
GARNISH: NONE

Tasting notes: sour, bitter, spicy, earthy

This straightforward cooler has something for everyone, checking just about every box one could possibly want in a beverage.

---

1 oz. black cherry juice

2 oz. chai concentrate

3 oz. cold-brew coffee

1 oz. Vanilla Syrup (see page 220)

2 dashes of El Guapo Chicory Pecan bitters

1   Place all of the ingredients in a cocktail shaker, fill it two-thirds of the way with ice, and shake vigorously until chilled.

2   Strain over crushed ice into the double rocks glass and enjoy.

FIRE EYES

GLASSWARE: HIGHBALL GLASS
GARNISH: NONE

Tasting notes: refreshing, tangy, sour, spicy

The Thai Chile Shrub is potent stuff, but two bitters, a touch of lime juice, and the hibiscus tea know how to put that strength to work.

3 oz. iced hibiscus tea

1 oz. Thai Chile Shrub (see page 216)

1 oz. fresh lime juice

6 drops of El Guapo Holiday Pie bitters

6 drops of El Guapo Polynesian Kiss bitters

1   Place all of the ingredients in a cocktail shaker, fill it two-thirds of the way with ice, and shake vigorously until chilled.

2   Strain over ice into the highball glass and enjoy.

RASTA LA VISTA

GLASSWARE: TUMBLER
GARNISH: NONE

Tasting notes: fruity, tropical, spicy, refreshing

A great one for those who love eclectic palate found in the world of tiki drinks.

1½ oz. iced hibiscus tea

1 oz. iced strawberry tea

½ oz. guava nectar

½ oz. fresh lime juice

½ oz. Cinnamon Syrup
(see page 191)

6 drops of El Guapo
Holiday Pie bitters

3 oz. grapefruit seltzer

1   Place all of the ingredients, except for the seltzer, in a cocktail shaker, fill it two-thirds of the way with ice, and shake vigorously until chilled.

2   Strain over ice into the tumbler, top with the seltzer, and enjoy.

PRIVATE PARADISE

GLASSWARE: HIGHBALL GLASS
GARNISH: EDIBLE ORCHID

Tasting notes: tropical, caramel, sour, summery

Foolproof and loaded with caramel flavor, the Burnt Sugar Syrup just may become your go-to sweetener when making drinks.

---

3 oz. iced hibiscus tea

1 oz. Burnt Sugar Syrup (see page 221)

½ oz. Grenadine (see page 197)

6 drops of El Guapo Holiday Pie bitters

½ oz. fresh lime juice

1   Place all of the ingredients in a cocktail shaker, fill it two-thirds of the way with ice, and shake vigorously until chilled.

2   Strain over ice into the highball glass, garnish with the edible orchid, and enjoy.

CHEGADA

GLASSWARE: HURRICANE GLASS
GARNISH: ORANGE WHEEL

Tasting notes: anise, sour, rich, effervescent

A good one to turn to following a delicious dinner enjoyed al fresco in the summer.

½ oz. fresh lemon juice

¼ oz. Grenadine (see page 197)

½ oz. fresh lime juice

½ oz. Demerara Syrup (see page 214)

3 oz. iced licorice tea

1 oz. Coffee Syrup (see page 189)

1 oz. seltzer

1 Place all of the ingredients, except for the seltzer, in a cocktail shaker, fill it two-thirds of the way with ice, and shake vigorously until chilled.

2 Strain over ice into the Hurricane glass and top with the seltzer.

3 Garnish with the orange wheel and enjoy.

NIGHTBIRD

GLASSWARE: HIGHBALL GLASS
GARNISH: NONE

Tasting notes: sweet, sour, earthy, tropical

Töst is a producer of sparkling tea blends that do a remarkable job at mimicking the flavor and feel of sparkling wines, making them capable of providing a lift to most any concoction.

1 oz. black cherry juice

2 oz. iced prickly pear tea

½ oz. Vanilla Syrup (see page 220)

1 oz. pineapple juice

2 oz. Töst Rosé

1   Place all of the ingredients, except for the Rosé, in a cocktail shaker, fill it two-thirds of the way with ice, and shake vigorously until chilled.

2   Strain over ice into the highball glass, top with the Rosé, and enjoy.

CALICO SKIES

GLASSWARE: ROCKS GLASS
GARNISH: FRESH MINT

Tasting notes: herbal, spicy, rich, tropical

The Vanilla Latte Syrup is a true game-changer, with a flavor that lies somewhere between an aged rum and an ideal cup of coffee.

---

10 to 15 fresh mint leaves, torn

1 oz. Vanilla Latte Syrup (see page 222)

½ oz. apricot nectar

½ oz. Honey & Cinnamon Syrup (see page 223)

½ oz. white grapefruit juice

1½ oz. pineapple juice

½ oz. fresh lime juice

1 teaspoon 10 percent Saline Solution (see page 195)

1 Place the mint leaves in a cocktail shaker and muddle.

2 Add ice and the remaining ingredients and shake vigorously until chilled.

3 Strain over crushed ice into the rocks glass, garnish with fresh mint, and enjoy.

Calico Skies, see page 121

THINKING OF YOU

GLASSWARE: BRANDY SNIFTER
GARNISH: PINEAPPLE CHUNK, FRESHLY GRATED NUTMEG

Tasting notes: rich, bitter, creamy, tropical

The rich mouthfeel provided by the Demerara Syrup and cream of coconut drastically lessens the bite of the other ingredients, which tend toward the acidic side of things.

---

1 oz. Demerara Syrup (see page 214)

1 oz. cold-brew coffee

1 oz. cream of coconut

1 oz. orange juice

4 oz. pineapple juice

1   Place all of the ingredients in a blender, add 5 oz. crushed ice, and puree until smooth.

2   Pour the drink into the brandy snifter, garnish with the pineapple chunk and nutmeg, and enjoy.

MR. OCTOBER

GLASSWARE: ROCKS GLASS
GARNISH: APPLE SLICES

Tasting notes: spicy, anise, autumnal

All of the flavors of fall, gathered in one package.

1½ oz. apple juice

½ oz. iced licorice tea

¾ oz. Cinnamon Syrup
(see page 191)

¾ oz. fresh lemon juice

2 dashes of El Guapo
Fuego bitters

1 Place all of the ingredients in a cocktail shaker, fill it two-thirds of the way with ice, and shake vigorously until chilled.

2 Double strain over ice into the rocks glass, garnish with the apple slices, and enjoy.

THE ISLAND

GLASSWARE: ROCKS GLASS
GARNISH: PINEAPPLE CHUNK

Tasting notes: refreshing, tropical, anise, herbal

The first few sips are akin to an escape—after that, you'll be in a clement place where the multiple layers of flavor can make their way to you.

---

1 oz. iced licorice tea

1 oz. iced spearmint tea

½ oz. Demerara Syrup (see page 214)

1 oz. pineapple juice

½ oz. fresh lemon juice

1 oz. Coconut Syrup (see page 224)

1   Place all of the ingredients in a cocktail shaker, fill it two-thirds of the way with ice, and shake vigorously until chilled.

2   Strain over ice into the rocks glass, garnish with the pineapple chunk, and enjoy.

The Island, see page 127

MYSTERY OF LOVE

GLASSWARE: ROCKS GLASS
GARNISH: PASSION FRUIT SLICE, FRESH MINT

Tasting notes: rich, tropical, almond, sour

A dessert, decadent drink inspired by the flavor of the famous French cake, baba au rhum.

---

2 oz. iced vanilla rooibos tea

1½ oz. heavy cream

1 oz. Orgeat (see page 210)

½ oz. fresh lemon juice

1¼ oz. passion fruit puree

½ oz. El Guapo Chicory Pecan bitters

1 Place all of the ingredients in a cocktail shaker, fill it two-thirds of the way with ice, and shake vigorously until chilled.

2 Double strain over ice into the rocks glass, garnish with the passion fruit slice and fresh mint, and enjoy.

PINK FLAMINGO

GLASSWARE: HIGHBALL GLASS
GARNISH: EDIBLE FLOWERS

Tasting notes: herbal, floral, refreshing, sweet

There is some of the sweetness that this drink's pinkish hue suggests—but there's also so much more.

½ oz. iced mint tea

1 oz. iced hibiscus tea

½ oz. pineapple juice

½ oz. Rose Syrup (see page 225)

½ oz. condensed milk

½ oz. cream of coconut

1   Place all of the ingredients in a blender, add 5 oz. crushed ice, and puree until smooth.

2   Pour the drink into the highball glass, garnish with the edible flowers, and enjoy.

HEADLESS HORSEMAN

GLASSWARE: TIKI MUG
GARNISH: EDIBLE ORCHID

Tasting notes: earthy, creamy, spicy

Next autumn, skip the long lines at the cafe and the sugary pumpkin spice lattes and make this one your regular afternoon treat.

1½ oz. Pumpkin Syrup (see page 226)

¾ oz. cream of coconut

¾ oz. coconut milk

1 oz. iced vanilla almond tea

½ oz. Bali Spice Syrup (see page 212)

¾ oz. fresh orange juice

¾ oz. fresh lime juice

1 Place all of the ingredients in a blender, add 5 oz. crushed ice, and puree until smooth.

2 Pour the drink into the tiki mug and top with more crushed ice.

3 Garnish with the edible orchid and enjoy.

DAUPHIN

GLASSWARE: HIGHBALL GLASS
GARNISH: CACAO NIBS, STAR ANISE POD

Tasting notes: sweet, spicy, anise, chocolatey

Chocolate, coffee, and chiles go brilliantly together.

---

1 oz. Vanilla Latte Syrup (see page 222)

2 dashes of El Guapo Spiced Cocoa bitters

½ oz. Serrano Pepper Shrub (see page 227)

1 oz. iced licorice tea

1¼ oz. toasted coconut almond milk

1   Place all of the ingredients in a cocktail shaker, fill it two-thirds of the way with ice, and shake vigorously until chilled.

2   Strain over crushed or pebble ice into the highball glass, garnish with the cacao nibs and star anise, and enjoy.

GREEN GARDEN

GLASSWARE: DOUBLE ROCKS GLASS
GARNISH: LIME WHEEL, CUCUMBER RIBBON, TIKI UMBRELLA

Tasting notes: refreshing, sour, summery

Iced green apple tea is a powerful secret weapon for the mocktail mixologist, with a bright, sharp taste that can enliven straightforward serves.

---

1 oz. iced green apple tea

1 oz. cucumber juice

¾ oz. fresh lime juice

¾ oz. cream of coconut

1 Place all of the ingredients in a cocktail shaker, fill it two-thirds of the way with ice, and shake vigorously until chilled.

2 Strain over ice into the double rocks glass, garnish with the lime wheel, cucumber ribbon, and tiki umbrella, and enjoy.

THE ROBIN'S NEST

GLASSWARE: HURRICANE GLASS
GARNISH: BRÛLÉED PINEAPPLE (SEE PAGE 86), MARASCHINO CHERRY

Tasting notes: tart, spicy, rich, tropical

Passion Fruit Honey has such a unique sweet-and-sour character that you'll soon be searching for ways to work it into a beverage.

⅓ oz. Vanilla Syrup (see page 220)

½ oz. Cinnamon Syrup (see page 191)

1 oz. cold-brew coffee

½ oz. fresh lemon juice

¾ oz. pineapple juice

1 oz. Passion Fruit Honey (see page 209)

1 oz. cranberry juice

1 Place all of the ingredients, except for the cranberry juice, in a cocktail shaker, fill it two-thirds of the way with ice, and shake vigorously until chilled.

2 Strain over crushed ice into the Hurricane glass and float the cranberry juice on top, pouring it slowly over the back of a spoon.

3 Garnish the mocktail with the Brûléed Pineapple and maraschino cherry and enjoy.

BRING ON THE BUBBLES

When the time comes to lift yourself above a dreary day, a few bubbles are all one needs to escape. Instantly refreshing and carrying an irresistible celebratory air, these sparkling drinks make the most of the effervescent elements we all love, from the variety of seltzers now on the market and standbys like club soda and ginger beer to inventive zero-proof offerings from companies such as Töst.

RASPBERRY, CHAMOMILE & LIME RICKEY

GLASSWARE: HIGHBALL GLASS
GARNISH: FRESH RASPBERRIES

Tasting notes: floral, berries, tart, refreshing

The honeyed flavor of chamomile keeps this one on the right side of being too tart.

---

2 oz. fresh lime juice

1 oz. Chamomile Syrup
(see page 219)

3 oz. Bottlegreen summer
raspberry cordial

2 oz. club soda

1   Place the lime juice, syrup, and cordial in a cocktail shaker, fill it two-thirds of the way with ice, and shake vigorously until chilled.

2   Strain over crushed ice into the highball glass and top with the club soda.

3   Garnish with the fresh raspberries and enjoy.

THAT'S MY NUMBER

GLASSWARE: TUMBLER
GARNISH: POMEGRANATE SEEDS, FRESH ROSEMARY

Tasting notes: tart, herbal, woody, spicy

No matter what kind of day you've had, this richly red mocktail will put a broad smile on your face.

---

1 oz. pomegranate juice

1 oz. cranberry juice

½ oz. fresh lime juice

½ oz. Rosemary Syrup (see page 202)

2 oz. ginger beer

1   Place all of the ingredients, except for the ginger beer, in a cocktail shaker, fill it two-thirds of the way with ice, and shake vigorously until chilled.

2   Strain over ice into the tumbler and top with the ginger beer.

3   Garnish with the pomegranate seeds and fresh rosemary and enjoy.

SUN RAYS LIKE STILTS

GLASSWARE: ROCKS GLASS
GARNISH: STRIP OF LEMON PEEL, MARASCHINO CHERRY

Tasting notes: sour, sweet, effervescent

A bright and elegant drink that will help you see the better side of those things that passed before you today.

---

1 oz. fresh lemon juice

1 teaspoon caster (superfine) sugar

2 oz. ginger ale

Dash of Grenadine (see page 197)

1   Place the lemon juice and sugar in the rocks glass and stir until the sugar has dissolved.

2   Add ice and the ginger ale and Grenadine and gently stir to combine.

3   Garnish with the strip of lemon peel and maraschino cherry and enjoy.

Sun Rays Like Stilts, see page 147

PRIVATEER

GLASSWARE: ROCKS GLASS
GARNISH: LIME WEDGE

Tasting notes: tropical, sweet

When a drink has as few ingredients as this one, you can be certain it's a winner.

½ oz. fresh lime juice

6 oz. cola

1 oz. Coconut Syrup (see page 224)

1 Add ice to the rocks glass, add all of the ingredients, and stir until chilled.

2 Garnish with the lime wedge and enjoy.

APPLE BLOSSOM

GLASSWARE: TUMBLER
GARNISH: CINNAMON STICK, STAR ANISE POD

Tasting notes: sweet, spicy, autumnal, creamy

Spiking cider with some vanilla and bubbles is a great way to switch things up once the crisp fall air descends.

Cinnamon, for the rim

Sugar, for the rim

3 oz. apple cider

Dash of Cinnamon Syrup (see page 191)

Dash of Vanilla Syrup (see page 220)

1 oz. cream soda

1   Place cinnamon and sugar in a dish and stir to combine. Wet the rim of the tumbler and coat it with the cinnamon sugar.

2   Place the apple cider and syrups in a cocktail shaker, fill it two-thirds of the way with ice, and shake vigorously until chilled.

3   Add ice to the glass, strain the drink over it, and top with the cream soda.

4   Garnish with the cinnamon stick and star anise and enjoy.

IT'S SO DIFFERENT HERE

GLASSWARE: HIGHBALL GLASS
GARNISH: RASPBERRIES, FRESH MINT

Tasting notes: bright, sour, fruity

A concoction that shows off how well raspberries pair with citrus.

½ oz. fresh lemon juice

½ oz. fresh lime juice

1 oz. Grenadine (see page 197)

1 oz. Raspberry Syrup (see page 204)

3 oz. club soda

1 Place the juices, Grenadine, and syrup in a cocktail shaker, fill it two-thirds of the way with ice, and shake vigorously until chilled.

2 Strain over ice into the highball glass and top with the club soda.

3 Garnish with the raspberries and fresh mint and enjoy.

SEASONS COME, SEASONS GO

GLASSWARE: TUMBLER
GARNISH: NONE

Tasting notes: sweet, vanilla, earthy

The rooibos grounds the sweet elements here, providing this mocktail with an unshakable foundation that can accommodate any number of riffs.

---

1 oz. peach nectar

1 oz. iced vanilla rooibos tea

½ oz. Vanilla Syrup (see page 220)

4 oz. seltzer

1   Place the peach nectar, iced tea, and syrup in a cocktail shaker, fill it two-thirds of the way with ice, and shake vigorously until chilled.

2   Strain over ice into the tumbler, top with the seltzer, and enjoy.

ONE FINE MORNING

GLASSWARE: CHAMPAGNE FLUTE
GARNISH: ORANGE WHEEL

Tasting notes: herbal, bright, effervescent

This brilliant take on the Mimosa just may change brunch forever.

---

2 oz. fresh orange juice

2 oz. Töst

1   Pour the orange juice into the Champagne flute and top with the Töst.

2   Garnish with the orange wheel and enjoy.

LET'S STAY TOGETHER

GLASSWARE: ROCKS GLASS
GARNISH: LIME WEDGE

Tasting notes: salty, bright, fruity

A simple spritzer that will keep you cool once the temperatures start to rise.

Salt, for the rim

½ oz. fresh lime juice

½ oz. fresh lemon juice

1 oz. Simple Syrup (see page 193)

4 oz. lemon-lime seltzer

1 Wet the rim of the rocks glass and coat it with salt.

2 Place the lime juice, lemon juice, and syrup in a cocktail shaker, fill it two-thirds of the way with ice, and shake vigorously until chilled.

3 Fill the rocks glass with ice and strain the drink over it.

4 Top with the seltzer, garnish with the lime wedge, and enjoy.

ASLEEP IN THE DESERT

GLASSWARE: DOUBLE ROCKS GLASS
GARNISH: FRESH MINT, CUCUMBER RIBBON

Tasting notes: tart, herbal, refreshing, vegetal

A sparkling limeade that captures the sensation of the delicious cool air that descends upon the desert once the sun goes down.

¼ oz. 10 Percent Saline Solution (see page 195)

2 fresh mint leaves

¼ cucumber, peeled and diced

2 oz. fresh lime juice

1 oz. Mint Syrup (see page 228)

3 oz. tonic water

1 Place the saline solution, mint, and cucumber in a cocktail shaker and muddle.

2 Add ice, the lime juice, and syrup and shake vigorously until chilled.

3 Double strain over ice into the double rocks glass and top with the tonic.

4 Garnish with fresh mint and the cucumber ribbon and enjoy.

Asleep in the Desert, see page 161

THE MORNING AFTER

GLASSWARE: WINEGLASS
GARNISH: ORANGE WHEEL

Tasting notes: rich, sweet, revitalizing, floral

When you want to take it easy following a long night, this playful serve has you covered.

---

2 teaspoons orange marmalade

1 oz. fresh lime juice

½ oz. fresh blood orange juice

½ oz. maple syrup

2 oz. club soda

1   Place all of the ingredients, except for the club soda, in a cocktail shaker, fill it two-thirds of the way with ice, and shake vigorously until chilled.

2   Double strain over ice into the wineglass and top with the club soda.

3   Garnish with the orange wheel and enjoy.

ESPERANZA

GLASSWARE: HIGHBALL GLASS
GARNISH: NONE

Tasting notes: spicy, herbal, berries, tart

Letting the three ingredients that form the base of this drink get acquainted in the refrigerator for an hour does wonders for the finished product.

½ jalapeño chile pepper, seeds removed

½ cup raspberries

½ oz. fresh lemon juice

3 oz. Töst Rosé

1 Place the jalapeño, raspberries, and lemon juice in a cocktail shaker and muddle. Let the mixture macerate in the refrigerator for 1 hour.

2 Add ice to the cocktail shaker and shake vigorously until chilled.

3 Double strain over ice into the highball glass, top with the Töst Rosé, and enjoy.

TWISTED TEMPLE

GLASSWARE: HIGHBALL GLASS
GARNISH: MARASCHINO CHERRY

Tasting notes: spicy, sweet, sour

A slightly souped-up, more mature version of the classic Shirley Temple.

1½ oz. Grenadine (see page 197)

2 oz. Lemon-Lime Juice (see page 194)

½ oz. Simple Syrup (see page 193)

3 oz. ginger beer

1. Place the Grenadine, Lemon-Lime Juice, and syrup in a cocktail shaker, fill it two-thirds of the way with ice, and shake vigorously until chilled.

2. Strain over ice into the highball glass and top with the ginger beer.

3. Garnish with the maraschino cherry and enjoy.

Twisted Temple, see page 167

TAMALPAIS

GLASSWARE: ROCKS GLASS
GARNISH: STRIP OF ORANGE PEEL

Tasting notes: sour, tropical, bright, buttery

The beguiling flavor of tamarind, which moves from sweet to citrus to buttery all in a single sip, keys this concoction.

¼ oz. Tamarind Syrup (see page 229)

½ oz. fresh lemon juice

½ oz. black cherry juice

3 oz. club soda

2 dashes of El Guapo Polynesian Kiss bitters

1   Place the syrup and juices in a cocktail shaker, fill it two-thirds of the way with ice, and shake vigorously until chilled.

2   Strain over ice into the rocks glass and top with the club soda and bitters.

3   Garnish with the strip of orange peel and enjoy.

MIGHT AS WELL BE SPRING

GLASSWARE: ROCKS GLASS
GARNISH: FRESH MINT, PEACH WEDGE

Tasting notes: spicy, earthy, fruity, herbal

A good one to make a pitcher of and set out for Easter, Mother's Day, or a late spring brunch.

½ oz. Ginger Syrup (see page 199)

2 oz. peach nectar

1½ oz. Passion Fruit Honey (see page 209)

6 fresh mint leaves, torn

2 oz. club soda

1 Place all of the ingredients, except for the club soda, in a cocktail shaker and muddle.

2 Add ice and shake vigorously until chilled.

3 Double strain over ice into the rocks glass and top with the club soda.

4 Garnish with fresh mint and the peach wedge and enjoy.

Might as well be Spring, see page 171

BLANKET ON THE GROUND

GLASSWARE: HIGHBALL GLASS
GARNISH: LIME WEDGE, FRESH MINT

Tasting notes: tropical, spicy, tart

A drink to sit out under the stars on a summer's night and dream with.

1½ oz. Bali Spice Syrup
(see page 212)

1½ oz. fresh lime juice

1 oz. coconut milk

3 oz. ginger beer

1 Place the syrup, lime juice, and coconut milk in a cocktail shaker, fill it two-thirds of the way with ice, and shake vigorously until chilled.

2 Strain over ice into the highball glass and top with the ginger beer.

3 Garnish with the lime wedge and fresh mint and enjoy.

LET IT RIDE

GLASSWARE: ROCKS GLASS
GARNISH: FRESH FIG

Tasting notes: fruity, rich, herbal, earthy

The white tea in the Rosé brightens a quartet of dark, bold ingredients.

---

1 oz. black cherry juice

½ oz. Licorice Syrup (see page 231)

½ oz. Fig Leaf Syrup (see page 232)

2 oz. Töst Rosé

6 drops of El Guapo Chicory Pecan bitters

1   Place the juice and syrups in a cocktail shaker, fill it two-thirds of the way with ice, and shake vigorously until chilled.

2   Strain over ice into the rocks glass and top with the Rosé and bitters.

3   Garnish with the fresh fig and enjoy.

SATURDAY SUN

GLASSWARE: CHAMPAGNE FLUTE
GARNISH: LEMON TWIST

Tasting notes: sour, floral, refreshing

Bottlegreen makes a whole line of cordials that are well worth checking out for the mocktail enthusiast.

---

1 tablespoon caster (superfine) sugar

1 oz. fresh lemon juice

3 oz. Bottlegreen elderflower cordial, chilled

2 oz. seltzer

1 Place the sugar and lemon juice in a cocktail shaker and dry shake until the sugar has dissolved.

2 Strain into the Champagne flute and top with the elderflower cordial and seltzer.

3 Garnish with the lemon twist and enjoy.

BEAU SOIR

GLASSWARE: ROCKS GLASS
GARNISH: ORANGE WEDGE

Tasting notes: bright, spicy, tropical

As elegant and moving as the Debussy song that serves as its namesake.

½ oz. fresh lemon juice

½ oz. fresh orange juice

1 oz. Vanilla & Chile Syrup (see page 230)

1 oz. Passion Fruit Honey (see page 209)

3 oz. seltzer

1 Place all of the ingredients, except for the seltzer, in a cocktail shaker, fill it two-thirds of the way with ice, and shake vigorously until chilled.

2 Strain over ice into the rocks glass and top with the seltzer.

3 Garnish with the orange wedge and enjoy.

Beau Soir, see page 179

LOVE & LIGHT

GLASSWARE: TUMBLER
GARNISH: NONE

Tasting notes: spicy, sour, rich

Cherry juice and chai concentrate may seem like an unlikely pair, but, as you will see, each has more than enough depth to be accommodating.

1½ oz. black cherry juice

1½ oz. chai concentrate

1 oz. Vanilla & Chile Syrup (see page 230)

2 dashes of El Guapo Holiday Pie bitters

2 dashes of El Guapo Love Potion bitters

½ oz. fresh lime juice

2 oz. cranberry lime seltzer

1 Place all of the ingredients, except for the seltzer, in a cocktail shaker, fill it two-thirds of the way with ice, and shake vigorously until chilled.

2 Strain over ice into the tumbler, top with the seltzer, and enjoy.

SUMMER CAME EARLY

GLASSWARE: HIGHBALL GLASS
GARNISH: PINEAPPLE LEAVES, LIME WEDGE

Tasting notes: refreshing, bright, tropical

Yuzu, with its intense and wide-ranging citrus flavor, is worth considering as a substitute in any drink featuring lemon or grapefruit juice.

½ oz. Vanilla Syrup (see page 220)

½ oz. fresh orange juice

½ oz. yuzu juice

½ oz. Grenadine (see page 197)

1 oz. pineapple juice

2 oz. ginger beer

1 Place all of the ingredients, except for the ginger beer, in a cocktail shaker, fill it two-thirds of the way with ice, and shake vigorously until chilled.

2 Strain over crushed ice into the highball glass and top with the ginger beer.

3 Garnish with pineapple leaves and the lime wedge and enjoy.

QUIET STORM

GLASSWARE: HIGHBALL GLASS
GARNISH: NONE

Tasting notes: sour, tropical, sweet, spicy

Tart and tangy, the Rhubarb Syrup serves as a perfect foil for numerous sweet elements in this one.

¾ oz. pineapple juice

½ oz. fresh lime juice

½ oz. Rhubarb Syrup (see page 233)

½ oz. Honey & Ginger Syrup (see page 190)

½ oz. Grenadine (see page 197)

2 oz. cola

1   Place all of the ingredients, except for the cola, in a cocktail shaker, fill it two-thirds of the way with ice, and shake vigorously until chilled.

2   Strain over ice into the highball glass, top with the cola, and enjoy.

APPENDIX

COFFEE SYRUP

1 cup water

2¼ oz. brewed espresso

Dash of cinnamon

Dash of chili powder

2 cups sugar

1 Place the water, espresso, cinnamon, and chili powder in a saucepan and bring the mixture to a boil, stirring occasionally.

2 Add the sugar and stir until it has dissolved.

3 Remove the pan from heat and let the syrup cool.

4 Strain the syrup before using or storing in the refrigerator, where it will keep for up to 1 month.

HONEY & GINGER SYRUP

2 cups honey

2 cups water

2⅔ oz. fresh ginger, minced

3 oz. fresh orange juice

1   Place all of the ingredients in a blender and puree until smooth.

2   Strain the syrup before using or storing in the refrigerator.

CINNAMON SYRUP

1 cup water

2 cinnamon sticks, halved

2 cups sugar

1 Place the water and cinnamon sticks in a saucepan and bring the mixture to a boil.

2 Add the sugar and stir until it has dissolved. Remove the pan from heat.

3 Cover the pan and let the syrup sit at room temperature for 12 hours.

4 Strain the syrup through cheesecloth before using or storing in the refrigerator, where it will keep for up to 1 month.

CHOCOLATE GANACHE

½ lb. chocolate

1 cup heavy cream

1   Place the chocolate in a heatproof mixing bowl and set aside.

2   Place the heavy cream in a small saucepan and bring to a simmer over medium heat.

3   Pour the cream over the chocolate and let the mixture rest for 1 minute.

4   Gently whisk the mixture until thoroughly combined. Use immediately or store in the refrigerator.

SIMPLE SYRUP

1 cup water

1 cup sugar

1   Place the water in a saucepan and bring it to a boil.

2   Add the sugar and stir until it has dissolved.

3   Remove the pan from heat and let the syrup cool before using or storing in the refrigerator, where it will keep for up to 3 months.

LEMON-LIME JUICE

1 (16 oz.) bottle of Santa Cruz 100 percent lime juice

1 (16 oz.) bottle of Santa Cruz 100 percent lemon juice

1 Place the juices in a large container and shake vigorously to combine. Use immediately or store in the refrigerator.

10 PERCENT SALINE SOLUTION

1 oz. salt

Warm water, as needed

1 Place the salt in a mason jar and add warm water until the mixture measures 10 oz.

2 Stir to combine and let the solution cool before using or storing.

SWEET & SOUR

2 oz. fresh lemon juice

4 oz. fresh lime juice

6 oz. Demerara Syrup
(see page 214)

1   Place all of the ingredients in a
    mason jar, seal it, and shake until
    combined.

2   Use immediately or store in the
    refrigerator, where it will keep for up
    to 3 months.

GRENADINE

2 cups 100 percent
pomegranate juice

2 cups sugar

1   Place the pomegranate juice in a saucepan and bring it to a simmer over medium-low heat. Cook until it has reduced by half.

2   Add the sugar and stir until it has dissolved.

3   Remove the pan from heat and let the grenadine cool completely before using or storing in the refrigerator.

CASHEW ORGEAT

1 cup cashew milk

2 cups sugar

1 teaspoon orange
blossom water

1   Place the cashew milk in a saucepan
and bring it to a simmer.

2   Place the sugar in a large mason jar,
pour the warm cashew milk over the
sugar, and stir until it has dissolved.
Let the mixture cool.

3   Stir in the orange blossom water
and use immediately or store in the
refrigerator.

GINGER SYRUP

1 cup water

1 cup sugar

2-inch piece of fresh ginger, unpeeled and chopped

1 Place the water in a saucepan and bring it to a boil.

2 Add the sugar and stir until it has dissolved.

3 Stir in the ginger, remove the pan from heat, and let the syrup cool.

4 Strain the syrup before using or storing in the refrigerator, where it will keep for up to 1 month.

BASIL SYRUP

1 cup water

1 cup sugar

12 fresh basil leaves

1 Place the water in a saucepan and bring it to a boil.

2 Add the sugar and stir until it has dissolved.

3 Stir in the basil, remove the pan from heat, and let the syrup cool completely.

4 Strain the syrup before using or storing in the refrigerator.

CUCUMBER SYRUP

1 cup freshly pressed
cucumber juice

1 cup caster (superfine)
sugar

1   Place the ingredients in a blender
    and puree until the sugar has
    dissolved. Use immediately or store
    in the refrigerator.

ROSEMARY SYRUP

1 cup water

1 cup sugar

4 sprigs of fresh rosemary

1   Place the water in a saucepan and bring to a boil.

2   Add the sugar and rosemary and stir until the sugar has dissolved.

3   Remove the pan from heat and let the syrup cool completely.

4   Strain before using or storing.

THYME SYRUP

1 cup water

1 cup sugar

6 sprigs of fresh thyme

1 Place the water in a saucepan and bring to a boil.

2 Add the sugar and thyme and stir until the sugar has dissolved.

3 Remove the pan from heat and let the syrup cool completely.

4 Strain before using or storing.

RASPBERRY SYRUP

1 cup water

1 cup sugar

20 fresh raspberries

1 Place the water in a saucepan and bring to a boil.

2 Add the sugar and raspberries and cook, mashing the raspberries and stirring the syrup, for 5 minutes.

3 Remove the pan from heat and let the syrup cool completely.

4 Strain before using or storing.

LAVENDER SYRUP

1 cup water

1½ cups sugar

Handful of dried lavender buds

1 Place the water in a saucepan and bring to a boil.

2 Add the sugar and stir until the sugar has dissolved.

3 Remove the pan from heat, stir in the lavender, and let the syrup cool completely.

4 Strain before using or storing.

AGAVE SYRUP

¾ cup agave nectar

¼ cup water

1 Place the ingredients in a saucepan and bring to a simmer. Cook until the syrup has the desired consistency.

2 Remove the pan from heat and let the syrup cool completely before using or storing.

RASPBERRY & THYME SHRUB

½ cup sugar

½ cup white wine vinegar

½ cup raspberries

2 tablespoons thyme

1 Place all of the ingredients in a saucepan and bring to a simmer, mashing the raspberries and stirring to dissolve the sugar.

2 Cook for 5 minutes, remove the pan from heat, and strain the shrub into a mason jar. Let the shrub cool completely before using or storing.

BANANA SYRUP

2 bananas, peeled and sliced

1 cup sugar

½ cup water

Pinch of fine sea salt

1 Place the bananas and sugar in a saucepan, stir until the bananas are coated, and let them macerate for 3 hours.

2 Add the water and salt and bring the mixture to a boil over medium heat, stirring to dissolve the sugar.

3 Remove the pan from heat and let the syrup cool. Strain the syrup before using or storing in the refrigerator, where the syrup will keep for up to 1 month.

PASSION FRUIT HONEY

1 cup honey

1 cup passion fruit puree

1   Place the honey in a saucepan and warm it over medium heat until it is runny.

2   Pour the honey into a mason jar, stir in the passion fruit puree, and let the mixture cool before using or storing in the refrigerator, where it will keep for up to 1 month.

ORGEAT

2 cups almonds

1 cup Demerara Syrup
(see page 214)

1 teaspoon orange
blossom water

1   Preheat the oven to 400°F. Place the
    almonds on a baking sheet, place
    them in the oven, and toast until
    they are fragrant, about 5 minutes.
    Remove the almonds from the oven
    and let them cool completely.

2   Place the nuts in a food processor
    and pulse until they are a coarse
    meal. Set the almonds aside.

3   Place the syrup in a saucepan and
    warm it over medium heat. Add the
    almond meal, remove the pan from
    heat, and let the mixture steep for
    6 hours.

4   Strain the mixture through
    cheesecloth and discard the solids.
    Stir in the orange blossom water
    and use immediately or store in the
    refrigerator.

HIBISCUS SYRUP

¼ cup dried hibiscus blossoms

2 cups Demerara Syrup (see page 214)

1 Place the hibiscus blossoms and syrup in a large mason jar and let the mixture steep at room temperature for 6 hours.

2 Strain the syrup and use immediately or store in the refrigerator.

BALI SPICE SYRUP

3 cinnamon sticks, crushed

12 whole cloves

12 star anise pods

2 cups honey

1 Place the cinnamon sticks, cloves, and star anise in a spice grinder and grind until the spices are fine, about 1 minute.

2 Place the ground spices in a saucepan and toast them over medium heat until they are aromatic, shaking the pan continually.

3 Add the honey, bring the mixture to a boil, and then reduce the heat and simmer for 5 minutes. Turn off the heat and let the syrup cool for about 1 hour.

4 Scrape the bottom of the pan to get all of the little seasoning bits and strain the syrup through a mesh strainer or chinois, using a spatula to help push the syrup through. Use immediately or store in the refrigerator.

MOLASSES SYRUP

1 cup water

2 cups sugar

½ cup molasses

1   Place the water in a saucepan and bring it to a boil.

2   Add the sugar and stir until it has dissolved.

3   Stir in the molasses, remove the pan from heat, and let the syrup cool completely before using or storing.

DEMERARA SYRUP

1 cup water

½ cup demerara sugar

1½ cups sugar

1   Place the water in a saucepan and bring it to a boil.

2   Add the sugars and stir until they have dissolved. Remove the pan from heat and let the syrup cool completely before using or storing.

HERB TEA

2 tablespoons fresh rosemary

2 tablespoons fresh thyme

2 tablespoons fresh oregano

2 teaspoons freshly ground black pepper

2 cups boiling water

1 Place all of the ingredients in a mason jar, stir to combine, and let the mixture steep overnight.

2 Strain before using or storing.

THAI CHILE SHRUB

8 Thai chile peppers

½ cup cane vinegar

½ cup cane sugar

1   Place all of the ingredients in a saucepan and bring to a boil. Cook for 5 minutes, stirring to dissolve the sugar.

2   Remove the pan from heat and let the shrub cool completely.

3   Strain before using or storing.

PEAR & CARDAMOM HORCHATA

3½ cinnamon sticks

14 green cardamom pods

¾ nutmeg seed

7 cups pear juice

4 cups water

4¼ cups jasmine rice

1 lb. honey

1 vanilla bean

Zest of 1 lime

Cinnamon Syrup (see page 191), as needed

1 Preheat the oven to 350°F. Place the cinnamon sticks, cardamom pods, and nutmeg seed on a baking sheet, place it in the oven, and toast the spices for 20 minutes. Remove them from the oven and let them cool.

2 Place the pear juice, water, rice, honey, vanilla bean, lime zest, and toasted aromatics in a large container and let the mixture steep at room temperature overnight.

3 Working in batches, place the mixture in a food processor and blitz until smooth. Double strain the mixture, pressing down on the solids to extract as much liquid as possible.

4 For every 4 cups of horchata, stir in 2 oz. of Cinnamon Syrup. Use immediately or store in the refrigerator, where the horchata will keep for up to 1 week.

RICH SIMPLE SYRUP

1 cup water

2 cups sugar

1 Place the water in a saucepan and bring it to a boil.

2 Add the sugar and cook, stirring continually, until it has dissolved.

3 Remove the pan from heat and let the syrup cool completely before using or storing.

CHAMOMILE SYRUP

1 cup water

2 cups sugar

5 bags of chamomile tea

1 Place the water in a saucepan and bring to a boil.

2 Add the sugar and stir until it has dissolved.

3 Add the tea, remove the pan from heat, and let the syrup steep as it cools.

4 Strain the syrup before using or storing in the refrigerator.

VANILLA SYRUP

1 cup water

2 cups sugar

1 vanilla bean

1 Place the water in a small saucepan and bring to a boil.

2 Add the sugar and stir until it has dissolved. Remove the pan from heat.

3 Halve the vanilla bean and scrape the seeds into the syrup. Cut the vanilla bean pod into thirds and add them to the syrup. Stir to combine, cover the pan, and let it sit at room temperature for 12 hours.

4 Strain the syrup through cheesecloth before using or storing in the refrigerator.

BURNT SUGAR SYRUP

1 cup sugar

½ cup water, at room temperature

½ cup warm water

1 Place the sugar and room-temperature water in a saucepan and bring to a boil over medium-high heat, stirring constantly, until the mixture becomes caramel-colored.

2 Remove the pan from heat, add the warm water —carefully, because the syrup will steam and bubble— and stir to incorporate. Let the syrup cool completely before using or storing.

VANILLA LATTE SYRUP

½ cup water

½ cup cold-brew coffee

1 cup demerara sugar

1 vanilla bean

1 Place the water and coffee in a saucepan and bring to a boil.

2 Add the sugar and stir until it has dissolved.

3 Halve the vanilla bean and scrape the seeds into the syrup. Cut the vanilla bean pod into thirds and add them to the syrup. Stir to combine, cover the pan, and let it sit at room temperature for 12 hours.

4 Strain the syrup through cheesecloth before using or storing in the refrigerator.

HONEY & CINNAMON SYRUP

1 cup water

2 cinnamon sticks, halved

1 cup honey

1 Place the water and cinnamon sticks in a saucepan and bring the mixture to a boil.

2 Add the honey and stir until it has liquefied. Remove the pan from heat.

3 Cover the pan and let the syrup sit at room temperature for 12 hours.

4 Strain the syrup through cheesecloth before using or storing in the refrigerator.

COCONUT SYRUP

1 cup coconut water

1 cup demerara sugar

1 Place the coconut water in a saucepan and bring it to a boil.

2 Add the sugar and stir until it has dissolved. Remove the pan from heat and let the syrup cool.

3 Use immediately or store in the refrigerator.

ROSE SYRUP

1 cup rose water

1 cup sugar

1 Place the rose water in a saucepan and bring to a boil.

2 Add the sugar and stir until it has dissolved. Remove the pan from heat and let the syrup cool.

3 Use immediately or store in the refrigerator.

PUMPKIN SYRUP

1 cup water

1 cup demerara sugar

1 cup pumpkin puree

1 Place the water in a saucepan and bring it to a boil.

2 Add the sugar and stir until it has dissolved.

3 Stir in the pumpkin puree and cook for 1 minute, stirring continually. Remove the pan from heat and let the syrup cool completely.

4 Strain the syrup before using or storing in the refrigerator.

SERRANO PEPPER SHRUB

4 serrano chile peppers

½ cup apple cider vinegar

½ cup sugar

1 Place all of the ingredients in a saucepan and bring to a boil. Cook for 5 minutes, stirring to dissolve the sugar.

2 Remove the pan from heat and let the shrub cool completely.

3 Strain before using or storing.

MINT SYRUP

1 cup water

1 cup sugar

12 fresh mint leaves

1 Place the water in a saucepan and bring it to a boil.

2 Add the sugar and stir until it has dissolved.

3 Stir in the mint, remove the pan from heat, and let the syrup cool completely

4 Strain the syrup before using or storing in the refrigerator.

TAMARIND SYRUP

1 cup water

1 cup sugar

¼ cup tamarind pulp

1 Place the water in a saucepan and bring to a simmer.

2 Add the sugar and tamarind pulp and stir until the sugar has dissolved and the tamarind has been incorporated.

3 Remove the pan from heat and let the mixture cool completely.

4 Strain before using or storing.

VANILLA & CHILE SYRUP

1 cup water

2 cups demerara sugar

2 jalapeño chile peppers, chopped

2 vanilla beans

1   Place the water in a saucepan and bring to a boil.

2   Add the demerara sugar and stir until it has dissolved.

3   Remove the pan from heat and stir in the jalapeños. Halve the vanilla beans, scrape the seeds into the syrup, and add the pods as well. Stir to combine and let the syrup cool completely.

4   Strain the syrup before using or storing in the refrigerator.

LICORICE SYRUP

1 cup water

1 cup sugar

1½ licorice roots

1 Place the water in a saucepan and bring to a boil.

2 Add the sugar and stir until it has dissolved.

3 Pour the syrup into a mason jar, add the licorice roots, and let the syrup cool completely.

4 Seal the mason jar and store the syrup in a cool dark place for 1 week.

5 Strain before using or storing.

FIG LEAF SYRUP

30 fig leaves

3 cups Simple Syrup (see page 193), warm

1 Place the fig leaves in a container and pour the Simple Syrup over them. Steep for 30 minutes.

2 Strain before using or storing.

RHUBARB SYRUP

1 cup rhubarb puree

2 cups sugar

2 cups water

Zest of ½ lemon

1   Place all of the ingredients in a saucepan and bring the mixture to a boil, stirring to dissolve the sugar.

2   Remove the pan from heat and let the syrup cool completely.

3   Strain the syrup before using or storing in the refrigerator, where it will keep for up to 1 month.

METRIC CONVERSIONS

U.S. Measurement	Approximate Metric Liquid Measurement	Approximate Metric Dry Measurement
1 teaspoon	5 ml	5 g
1 tablespoon or ½ ounce	15 ml	14 g
1 ounce or ⅛ cup	30 ml	29 g
¼ cup or 2 ounces	60 ml	57 g
⅓ cup	80 ml	76 g
½ cup or 4 ounces	120 ml	113 g
⅔ cup	160 ml	151 g
¾ cup or 6 ounces	180 ml	170 g
1 cup or 8 ounces or ½ pint	240 ml	227 g
1½ cups or 12 ounces	350 ml	340 g
2 cups or 1 pint or 16 ounces	475 ml	454 g
3 cups or 1½ pints	700 ml	680 g
4 cups or 2 pints or 1 quart	950 ml	908 g

INDEX

ABOUT
CIDER MILL PRESS
BOOK PUBLISHERS

Great ideas grow over time. From seed to harvest,
Appleseed Press brings fine reading and entertainment
together between the covers of its creatively crafted
books. Our grove bears fruit twice a year, publishing
a new crop of titles each spring and fall.

"Where Good Books Are Ready for Press"

501 Nelson Place
Nashville, Tennessee 37214

cidermillpress.com